T0198767

Day, Dusk, or Night

Written by:
Marie Matthews

Illustrated by:
EA Mabagos

Balboa Press books may be ordered through booksellers or by contacting:

Balboa Press
A Division of Hay House
1663 Liberty Drive
Bloomington, IN 47403
www.balboapress.com
844-682-1282

ISBN: 978-1-9822-7663-8 (sc)
ISBN: 978-1-9822-7665-2 (hc)
ISBN: 978-1-9822-7664-5 (e)

Library of Congress Control Number: 2021922271

Print information available on the last page.

Balboa Press rev. date: 11/15/2021

BALBOA.PRESS
A DIVISION OF HAY HOUSE

For my children. May you see your beauty reflected in these pages. I love you so very much. I truly am the luckiest momma!

Sometimes when we worry,
We're scared, or we fret,
It becomes much too easy
For us to forget
That there are helpers we call
Who come day, dusk, or night.
They protect us and our spaces
And bring in God's light.

There's no problem too big.
There's no problem too small.
There's no problem that they
Cannot help with at all.

They are stronger than fear.
They are stronger than worry.
They are stronger than distractions
That cause us to flurry.

6

They help clear our energy
When we feel so-so.
They are stronger than darkness,
Sadness, and woe.

Call on Archangel Michael,
The warrior, the leader, the general of light.
He strikes fear into evil
With his sword, fire, and might.

He directs the Archangels
From his eagle eye view
And shields if you ask
With his royal hue.

He protects all God's children.
He's the calm in the storm.
His demeanor is
Especially caring and warm.

Call on Archangel Gabriel.
He's the spy who blends in.
His mission's to protect you
And ensure the light wins!

He's stealth as a ninja.
Like water he moves.
He clears sneaky energy
That hides in the grooves.

His lasery light helps you
Burn up the muck.
So you find the right words
When you're feeling stuck.

Call on Archangel Uriel
When you feel out of your body.
He keeps you centered on Earth
When your head gets too cloudy.

He brings clarity to chaos
When it's time to do battle.
He helps you release all your fears
And get back in the saddle.

He illuminates your brilliance
When it's shrouded in dark,
And brings it to light
With his Divine spark.

Call on Archangel Raphael,
The scientist, the doctor,
The resident healer.
He uses light to remove
Pesky energy stealers.

14

When you bring light into your body
With the air that you breathe,
Ask, and he will command
The darkness to leave.
Raphael's emerald light warms
From head to toes,
So forgiveness and beauty
Can heal all your woes.

Call on Archangel Metatron,
The pillar, the center,
The divine connection.
He clears your mind
For thought and reflection.

He helps you stand strong
When you are in doubt
And protects you from evil,
Both within and without.

His cube is an unbreakable
Shield of light
That clears your body and spaces
So you can take flight.

Call on Archangel Haniel,
The wizard, the alchemist,
The artful magician.
He uses his magic to bring
Peace to fruition.

He transforms evil
With wonder and joy
And shares his Divine magic
For you to employ.

He brings out your sparkle,
Converts darkness to light,
And ignites hope in your heart
So you lean in to the fight.

Sometimes when we worry,
We're scared, or we fret,
It becomes much too easy
For us to forget
That there are helpers we call
Who come anytime.
They protect us and our spaces
And bring in the Divine.

They're here to support you.
They defy time and space.
They can be everywhere and nowhere
And in more than one place.

So no matter your culture,
No matter your race,
No matter your gender,
Belief system, or faith.

They're here to protect you.
They bring in the light.
Ask for help and they'll be there,
Day, dusk, or night.

Using Light to Calm Your Feelings

Breathe in deeply as deeply as you can. Inhale light through your nose. Exhale through your mouth all that is bothering you or making you feel fearful. Visualize more and more light filling your body with each inhale. Release all that's not light with each exhale. Repeat this in sets of three until you feel better. Ask Archangel Michael to burn up all of that unwanted energy with his sword of fire and light.

Using Light to Calm Your Body

Breathe in deeply. Bring your breath all the way down to your toes. Breathe out. Try to push the air all the way out. Do this three times. Continue deep breathing. Now, focus on your feet. How do they feel? If you feel any discomfort, ask the archangels to send light to that area. Picture the light healing any discomfort. Now check in on your left leg, and send light there if it's needed. Do the same with your right leg. Keep going with each part of your body until you get all the way up to the top of your head. You can do this anytime and anywhere.

Prayer to the Archangels for Guidance & Protection

Follow your normal bedtime or morning routine. Add the below prayer before you go to sleep and before you start your day. Visualize the angels surrounding you as you say,

> Archangels, I ask for your protection and love. Fill me with light from God up above.
>
> Archangel Michael, please stand at my south.
>
> Archangel Gabriel, please stand at my west.
>
> Archangel Uriel, please stand at my north.
>
> Archangel Raphael, please stand at my east.
>
> Be with me in wake time and sleep time, all times day, dusk, and night. Help my highest good to come true and my dreams to take flight.
>
> Thank you! Thank you for your love, protection, and light.
>
> And so it is.

Author's Note

The Archangels are here to assist and protect anyone who asks for their help. Race, religion, socioeconomic class—none of these human constructs matter to them. Their love for God, for us as children of God and their duty to assist with our progression does.

My books are written with this in mind. It is key to the mental, emotional, and spiritual health and development of children that they see themselves reflected in the pages of books about spirituality so they can visualize and grow to know themselves as powerful, Divine beings of light.

Acknowledgments

A special thank-you to the illustrator, EA Mabagos, for his talent, grace, and willingness to make so many changes based on the feedback from community members. To each of the community members who analyzed illustrations and gave such personal feedback, your vulnerability, guidance, and love are deeply appreciated.

About the Author

Marie Matthews is a mother, a healer, and a teacher. Born an intuitive, as a child, Marie consistently connected with the Archangels for protection from unneeded and unwanted energy. It is this connection with the Archangels that continues to inspire Marie to embrace her own Divinity and follow her path. As a mother in a multiracial family and a teacher who works with children and teens from across the globe, Marie is passionate about empowering each child to discover, embrace, and love who they truly are as humans and encourage them to grow and Know Thyself and the Divine Light within.

Printed in the United States
by Baker & Taylor Publisher Services